Victorian Keighley Characters

by
IAN DEWHIRST

First Published 1990

Published by Hendon Publishing Co. Ltd.,
Hendon Mill, Nelson, Lancashire

Text © Ian Dewhirst, 1990

Printed by Peter Fretwell & Sons Ltd.,
Goulbourne Street, Keighley, West Yorkshire BD21 1PZ

Acknowledgements

My thanks are due to Stanley R. Boardman for Abraham Kershaw's scrapbook, Mr and Mrs C. E. Throup for original material on Matilda Florella Illingworth, Keighley Reference Library for photographs of Engine Billy, 'Pie' Leach and Bill o' th'Hoylus End, and the editors of the *Keighley News* and *Yorkshire Ridings Magazine*, in which several of these characters have previously appeared.

Ian Dewhirst

(1)   'William Hartley or Engine Billy, a clever half-wit'.

Introduction

The Victorian era bristled with characters. Many people then seemed little concerned about fitting themselves into a conventional pattern; they drew much of their interest and conversation from one another; they became familiar in their communities by virtue of their personalities or achievements, or simply by the jobs they did. 'If you're not good,' Keighley mothers would threaten about the 1870s, 'Bill Balk will fetch you!' Bill Balk being the pinder, supposedly not above stealing children and putting them in his pinfold! A similar idea of an over-zealous pinder had been expressed half a century earlier in verses on a predecessor, John Fustic:

> 'We've scarce a horse, or pig, or ass,
> But John has lugg'd its ear.'

Yet Victorian characters are not always easy to authenticate. I became interested some thirty years ago, when many veterans still remembered the later nineteenth century, and I soon filled a notebook with tales – which now I feel dubious about using. Too many old-timers described how, when young, they were taken to see Old Three Laps. They sounded sincere, they had plenty of details, but Old Three Laps had died in 1856 and demonstrably they never could have seen him.

Then there was a popular story about 'Pie' Leach being jostled whilst counting his sovereigns, one of which landed on top of Bill o' th'Hoylus End's hat. Passers-by scurried to help pick up the sovereigns, but Bill o' th'Hoylus stood as straight as a ramrod, saying, 'Well, ah'll be bahn nah, 'cos if ther's owt missin' tha'll nobbut blame me!' Unfortunately, each informant gave the tale a different setting – Church Green, High Street, Utley Cemetery, a barber's shop – and always my informant, or my informant's father, had been present. History can thus be seen to merge into folklore.

Many characters, once household names, have faded with their contemporaries' memories, leaving little or no written record; like tantalising William Hartley or Engine Billy, a clever half-wit said to have planned a railway across Ilkley Moor. He also thought he had discovered the principle of perpetual motion, by some patent juxtaposition of a pump, a reservoir and a water-wheel, though nobody gave it a trial. Just one hard fact about Engine Billy survives – he was allowed to study at the Keighley School of Art, 'by the kind indulgence of Mr T. C. Butterfield and Sir Swire Smith'. Possibly this tells us more about Mr T. C. Butterfield and Sir Swire Smith than about Engine Billy, although he did produce passable copies of a Rubens portrait and a window at Westminster Abbey.

On the other hand, all six characters chosen for this little book are verifiable in contemporary, if sometimes obscure, sources. Each illustrates a different type: the Depressive, the Publican, the Bard, the Politician, the Entrepreneur and the Prima Donna. All except the Depressive contributed towards the life of their period, leaving their community ultimately the richer for their efforts. The Politician and the Bard, and perhaps especially the Depressive, remain locally remembered, but the Publican, and quite tragically the Entrepreneur and the Prima Donna, are forgotten. It is hoped that the following pages will help, however briefly, to bring them back.

Keighley, June 1990.   Ian Dewhirst

The Depressive:

OLD THREE LAPS

The basic tale of Old Three Laps is soon told: real name William Sharp, of the Whorles Farm near Laycock, he suffered a disappointment in love in his thirtieth year, went to bed and remained there for forty-nine years, from 1807 till his death in 1856.

The circumstances are well authenticated. Within two years of his death, the book *Keighley, Past and Present* was devoting more than half its chapter on Laycock to Old Three Laps, cataloguing in prosaic detail the small downstairs room in which he had lain, with its stone-flagged floor, its fireplace only usable during certain weather conditions, its window patched up with wood where broken, its old clock minus weights and pendulum, covered with cobwebs, its small round table of dark oak; above all his plain four-poster bed without hangings. A fuller account followed in a pamphlet by Thomas Harrison, a Bingley printer, and by the 1880s the Rev. Sabine Baring-Gould was including him in *Yorkshire Oddities, Incidents and Strange Events*.

Let us first account for William Sharp's nickname, in reality inherited from his father, farmer, small worsted manufacturer and eccentric in his own right. Notorious for his niggardly ways, father Sharp once took a roll of cloth to the tailor to be made up into a coat, and the tailor remonstrated that unless he supplied more material the coat would have only three laps, or pleats. 'Then mak' it wi' three laps, or onyroad,' was the reply, and father and son were nicknamed for life.

Three Laps the younger was given much of his own way, was particularly fond of shooting, and for some years courted Mary Smith, a farmer's daughter from nearby Newsholme Dean. In 1807 the wedding date was arranged. A doggerel verse, one of several inspired by Old Three Laps, records the sad sequel:

'The father of Mary was ready with pride
To settle a dowry his daughter upon;
But vow'd that young 'Three Laps' should ne'er call her bride,
Should the father not equally portion his son.'

Local tradition elaborates to the extent of the prospective fathers-in-law quarrelling, Mary Smith being locked in her bedroom on her wedding day, Sharp going to church and returning home disappointed. Certainly, he got into bed and stayed there for the rest of his life.

One hesitates to challenge hallowed legend, but an 1839 account in the *Preston Chronicle* tells a different tale, 'The cause of his first taking to bed is said to be from his father having at two different times taken from him three guineas which he had saved, and on the second three guineas being taken from him, he declared he would never work any more, and took to his bed, which he has never since left.'

Whatever the reason, and despite a local tendency (across the safe distance of a hundred and fifty years) to view the situation as comic, there is surely tragedy in the lack of understanding of mental illness which could allow a physically healthy man in the prime of life to lie waste for half a century. The elder Sharp, who died in 1818, ensured by his will that poor William should always have a nurse to attend him.

Over the years, people flocked to the Whorles to look at Old Three Laps, creeping round the back of the house to peep in through his window. When he saw faces looking in at him, he would hide his head under the bedclothes. One little girl, remembering him vividly for the rest of her life, said he was 'like a big fat pig'. The *Preston Chronicle* described him as 'rolled up like a hedgehog'. Antiquarian William Scruton recalled him ('What a spectacle!') lying on his stomach 'rapidly counting his fingers as if trying to solve some problem or other. His long hair and beard (then quite grey) looked lank and neglected, and he wore nothing in the shape of a night-cap'. Although then in his seventies, Old Three Laps 'appeared stout and in good health'. Indeed, his appetite remained good, his flesh being 'firm, fair, and unwrinkled, save with fat'. His estimated weight was 240 lb.

A gentleman visitor, quoted by Baring-Gould, called him 'a mass of inanimate matter', and was minded of mad King Nebuchadnezzar; although, watching his nurse pull away the bedclothes, he thought he was kept scrupulously clean. In his later years at least, Three Laps' nurse was his aunt Sarah Marshall, a year older than himself.

The 1851 Census gives a succinct picture: 'William Sharp, Unmarried. Aged 74. Independent Landed Proprietor. Lain in bed 44 years.' 'His beard,' the *Preston Chronicle* adds, 'is grissly, his hair silvery white, and most enormous teeth project from his lips.'

Old Three Laps' few amusements included playing with his plate, when he had eaten his dinner, 'in the manner of a Chinese juggler, and with considerable ability', and extending his forefinger as though it were a gun and shooting at imaginary birds. When eating, he would roll over on to his knees, turn down the blankets and eat off the mattress, so that the crumbs should not get among the bedclothes. Although he would sometimes grunt like a pig when faced with visitors, he is said never to have spoken during those forty-nine years.

(2)   Old Three Laps in his bed – an artist's impression which embellished the front of Thomas Harrison's mid-Victorian pamphlet.

Towards the end of his life, his legs contracted and his appetite failed. He died on Monday morning, 3rd March, 1856. Just before he died, he spoke his one connected phrase in forty-nine years: 'Poor Bill, poor Bill, poor Bill Sharp!' A large crowd gathered to watch his funeral at Keighley Parish Church. The coffin resembled a big oak chest, and took eight men to lower it into the grave.

In his *By Moor and Fell* in 1899, Halliwell Sutcliffe, his tongue, one hopes, in his cheek, paid tribute to Old Three Laps, 'To go to bed was easy – but to stay there for nine-and-forty years! To lie and lie, years after one's anger had grown cool, and still to nurse the corpse of one's resentment, crushing the thought that, after all, one might be a fool for one's pains – yes, there was a touch of something near akin to genius in the man, and his memory lives at a day when many a worthier fellow has been forgotten.'

Perhaps, at the last, Old Three Laps had spoken his own best epitaph: 'Poor Bill, poor Bill, poor Bill Sharp!'

(3) 'A surviving photograph of Mrs Tap suggests that she could take a joke!'

The Publican:

HARRY TAP

On the March day in 1863 when the Prince of Wales married Princess Alexandra, Keighley's public holiday was enlivened by a procession. Fifty men rode through the streets in wagons and carts carrying porridge pans, cans and other household utensils. Afterwards they went into the Royal Oak Inn at Damside and sat down to a dinner of roast beef and nearly a hundredweight of plum pudding!

They were members of the Keighley Hen-Pecked Club, the pots and pans representing 'the insignia of their order'. Their dinner was provided by their Grand Master, landlord at the Royal Oak, who had decorated his hostelry for the occasion – across the street stretched an arch of evergreens and a strip of bunting bearing the legend 'Henpecked (please to think of the Club House) Society'. Over the door appeared the name by which the town knew him: Harry Tap.

Henry Hargreaves Thompson had come to Keighley from Colne in the 1840s as ostler at the Crown Inn, Church Green, later keeping the Fleece Tap behind Low Street. It was there that he earned his nickname Harry at Tap, shortened to Harry Tap. The name stuck with him when he became landlord at the Royal Oak.

With a characteristic eye for publicity, philanthropy and drollery, he was one of the first advertisers when the '*Keighley News*' started in 1862: 'HENRY THOMPSON, better known as HARRY TAP, wishes to inform the public that, owing to the old copper coinage being so cumbersome, he exchanges the old coin for new at any hour of the day, at the Royal Oak Inn, free of charge.'

He founded the Hen-Pecked Club about the same time, its rules comically couched in the language of the friendly societies with which he was also associated. Let a few examples illustrate their flavour:

'Every member of this Club shall work from six o'clock in the morning till nine at night, and fetch the various articles required for household management . . .'

'Resolved, that he shall go to bed exactly at ten o'clock, and rise at half-past five in the morning, in order to light the fire, sweep the hearth, and make everything ready for the reception of his wife . . .'

'Instead of the practice of joining a social company over a pint of good beer on a Saturday night, to enjoy himself, he shall black his own and wife's shoes, go errands, get his supper, and go to bed . . .'

'The best eatables of every description that can possibly be procured for money must be bought for his amiable wife, while he quietly sits down to a mess of oatmeal porridge, a plate of hasty pudding, or a red herring . . .'

'All the money which the utmost efforts of our industry can realize, shall be at our wives' disposal, for the purpose of pleasure trips to Morecambe Bay, or any other place . . .'

In other words, as their Club song expressed it:

'If man on earth would be respected,
Take this advice and don't neglect it –
If thou be strong and nothing ails thee,
Do whate'er thy wife shall tell thee;
Assist her in her household duty –
Remember she's thy chosen beauty.'

Members of the Hen-Pecked Club could hope for a measure of protection. So long as a husband was doing 'everything proper according to the Rules', he was not to be 'annoyed in his household duties by his wife, but be allowed to perform them in a manner worthy of the name of the Society'.

An unfairly scolded member could apply for the loan of a 'wife-taming cradle', invented by Harry Tap who had awarded himself a leather medal for it! This was six feet long by two feet wide, on big circular rockers, having 'a sliding board at the top, which will reach as far as the shoulders, and effectually prevents the occupant getting out'. It bore an inscription, 'Henpecked Club Peace Cradle, Box No. 6, Patent Cure for a Cross Wife'. The idea was for the husband to fasten his shrewish wife in it ('if the occupant be of small stature, some bolsters and cushions must be placed at the foot of the cradle, so as to keep her snugly in one position') and give her a rocking:

'Take my advice – it will not harm thee,
But on the other hand 'twill charm thee –
To Henry Thompson go thy ways, lad,
And get the cradle for three days, lad,
And rock therein thy charming beauty,
Till she comes round to do her duty.'

Of course, it was all in fun – there is no record of anybody actually using it – and lent itself to continuing jokes. 'Owing to the many applications for the cradle,' states an annual report of the Hen-Pecked Club, 'we have resolved that every member shall have it in his turn except in cases of urgent necessity.' It was even hoped that nobility

(4)   The wife-taming cradle of the Keighley Hen-Pecked Club.

would patronise the cradle, to say nothing of the French Emperor Louis Napoleon, 'he being the greatest henpecked member in Europe'.

Perhaps not surprisingly, when he founded his Hen-Pecked Club Harry Tap was still a bachelor; he did not marry until middle age.

It used to be the custom, each summer on the date of the Keighley Agricultural Show, to decorate streets and buildings, and the Royal Oak more than held its own. In 1864, for example, saw besides the usual flags and greenery, the cradle 'in an elevated position', with 'a man's effigy' so contrived as to keep it rocking. In 1865 the cradle floated on an adjoining dam, and contained a 'henpecked husband rocking the baby'. In 1868 the Royal Oak sported 'representations of the presidents of the hen-pecked clubs throughout the world, which had been painted expressly for the occasion by a local artist'.

Keighley must have felt a duller place when Harry Tap eventually married; although perhaps we should not speculate as to whether his changed status, or his leaving the Royal Oak for the less central King's Head in 1868, brought about the demise of the Hen-Pecked Club. Indeed, a surviving photograph of Mrs Tap suggests that she could take a joke!

Henry Hargreaves Thompson died aged 54 in 1877. By then he owned the White Horse Brewery in Halifax Road. 'His business habits made for him a position, and he died respected by a large circle of friends,' said his obituary. 'Commencing life with little or nothing, he amassed a considerable fortune by diligence and shrewdness in business, and by always attending to his own affairs.' He was president of the Keighley Licensed Victuallers' Association, member of the Conservative Club and the Sandywood Bowling Green Club. Though having no children of his own, he had been 'as a father to nephews and nieces, and a liberal giver to many charities'.

The Bard:

BILL O' TH'HOYLUS END

In July, 1897, a 61-year-old man lay dying in his sister's house in North Beck Terrace, Keighley. His doctor, a lover of literature, attempted to cheer him up by reciting a poem:

> 'Nivver dee i' thi shell, owd lad,
> Though some may laugh an' scorn;
> There wor nivver a neet afore ta neet,
> Bud what ther' com a morn;
> An' if blind forten used tha bad,
> Sho's happen noan so meean;
> Ta morn al come, an' then fer some
> The sun will shine ageean . . .'

The lines had been written by the dying man, but the poet was not to be roused. Soon afterwards he died.

'Self-indulgence, we have learned, spells self-destruction,' orated the minister at his funeral. 'During the nine years and more that I have known this my friend, so deep had he already got into the rut of habit that it was almost impossible for him to start on new ways.' Only his friends' generosity saved him from a pauper's grave.

William Wright, son of a weft manager of musical bent, had been born in 1836, in the Hoylus End houses at Hermit Hole; hence his nom de plume Bill o' th'Hoylus End. A rover in earlier life, and by turns soldier, sailor, puppeteer, actor and inventor, he eventually settled more or less to the trade of warp-dressing in his home town, although 'he only followed it at intervals'. He married and had children, but his domestic life (about which nothing is ever said) seems to have been unstable, and his declining years saw him dependent 'almost entirely upon the kindness of a good sister and the charity of friends'.

William Wright's standing as a writer has suffered from his reputation as a character, and a drinking one at that, as exemplified in his being remembered almost exclusively by his soubriquet. We shall pass over, here, such themes as his extravagant letters to Queen Victoria ('John Barleycorn has been my medical adviser') and his application for the post of Poet Laureate after the death of Tennyson; his wearing of Scotch cap and plaid to encourage a nickname, 'the

Yorkshire Burns'; and a galaxy of tales about South American war pigs at Haworth, and the like. We shall confine ourselves instead to a more sober view of a man too seldom considered as a writer.

Keighley, his source and background, grew in population from 11,000 to 36,000 in the decades between his birth and death. Local life expectancies stood, in his boyhood, at 36 years for a gentleman, 23 years for a mechanic, and 19 for a woolcomber; whilst at Haworth 41 out of every 100 babies died before the age of six. Even worse, if anything, was to come around mid-century, with a wholesale influx of destitute, desperate Irish. Yet Bill o' th'Hoylus's work would reflect, not simply the crudities of slum and factory life, but also that long, slow Victorian achievement of a kind of order out of chaos. He would celebrate his era's benefactors *(The Grand Old Man of Oakworth)* and its amenities *(The Opening of Devonshire Park)*.

His writing – prose and verse, dialect and standard English – was spectacularly uneven and varied. His sixteen-page *History o' Haworth Railway* came out in 1867, ran into innumerable editions and became a dialect classic. His *Howorth, Cowenheead, and Bogthorn Almenak* appeared annually through the 1870s; though the journals he had a hand in, *The Keighley Investigator* and *The Keighley Spectator*, were shorter-lived. The Lord Chamberlain banned his play, *The Wreck of the Bella.* His *Random Rhymes and Rambles* was published in 1876, a revised edition of his poems in 1891. Additionally, there were scores of topical penny pamphlets and broadsheets with titles like *Lines in Commemoration of the Anti-Vaccination Persecution and the Imprisonment of the Keighley Guardians, The Queen's Diamond Jubilee, The Keighley Cottage Hospital Gala, Lines Written During the Great Floods, 1896, Ahr New Mayor,* and ditties beginning 'Electors, Electors, be wise . . .'

Much of his work was, in the nature of Victorian pamphleteering, turned out at speed; as witness an occasion when he was fined ten shillings after an incident at the Crown Inn at Keighley: 'I set to work with my pen,' he would recount, 'and wrote a satire on the magistrate who took the most prominent part in dealing with my case. By the dinner hour on the following day, Saturday, I was in the market-place selling copies of the satire. People bought with avidity, and before Saturday went out I had disposed of a thousand copies at a penny each; which returns enabled me to pay the fine and then make a profit out of my prosecution.' Truly, a creative method conducive to ready vigour, but scarcely to literary polish!

Then there is the question of his literacy, and the extent to which other hands touched up his work before it reached the printers. On the

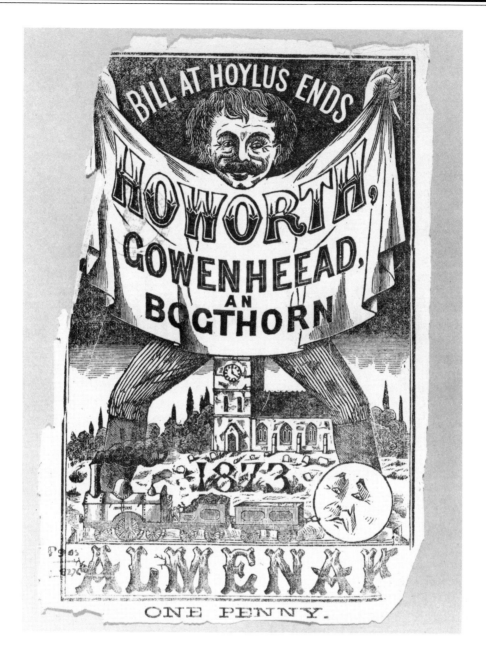

(5) The cover of the *'Howorth, Cowenheead, an Bogthorn Almenak'* for 1873. Its illustration suggests the Worth Valley Railway, old Haworth Church, and the moon whose reflection some Cowling (or Cowenheead) men are said to have tried to fish out of a dam in the belief that it was a cheese! It also contrives to give an impression of how Bill o' th'Hoylus End must have looked in his later thirties.

surface, Bill o' th'Hoylus End's life is fully chronicled, since in 1893, as a garrulous, aging man, he recorded his 'Adventures and Recollections' for a lengthy series in the *Keighley Herald* newspaper. Here his style reflects the competent but verbose journalism of the day, wherein he testifies to his youthful attendance at various homely educational establishments – one was in a thatched cottage and another had no regular teacher – before going to the Keighley National School till, he says, the age of fourteen. Yet his few surviving manuscripts seem to belie this amount of straightforward Victorian schooling:

'If a grand Pair of Boots walks down the Mane Street
its a 100 to one but ther on the wrong feet
or Should you get Treet to a pint of Rye ale
its down the wrong throyet it Shur to Sale.'

Indeed, this same *Adventures and Recollections* offers a comparison between what Bill o' th'Hoylus actually wrote, and what he was tidied into. Here is his published account of a hermit who lived in Holme House Wood during his boyhood:

'He (the hermit) once told my mother that he had more than once changed clothes with a scarecrow. Sometimes this queer person would never be seen by mortal man for months together, unless it were that I disturbed his solitude occasionally. Farmers often found occasion to complain of pillaging being carried on by night in their gardens and turnip fields.'

However, Bill o' th'Hoylus's tormented manuscript runs thus:

'I herd him tell my mother who was a kind harted warken woman that he had often Changed Clothing with the scarecrows and Some times for months together he would never be sene by mortel man unless with Such as my Self who invaded his Solitude allthough gardens or turnup feald often ware Plundred.'

The wordy style of the improved version ('unless it were', 'found occasion to complain') compares unfavourably with the terse colloquialism of the original.

A racy dialect vitality characterises his best writing; in standard English and in serious mood, Bill o' th'Hoylus End leaves much to be desired. Possibly an eye to patronage, and that 'charity of friends', coaxed him into subjects less suited to his talents, such as *Bonnie Cliffe Castle*, and *Ode to Sir Titus Salt* ('Go, string once more old Ebor's harp'), and *The Grand Old Man of Oakworth*, full of words like 'paean' and 'bard' and 'the Muse's call'; to say nothing of his embarrassing *In Memory of Thomas Ireland, Police Superintendent, Keighley. Born 1831, Died 1887*:

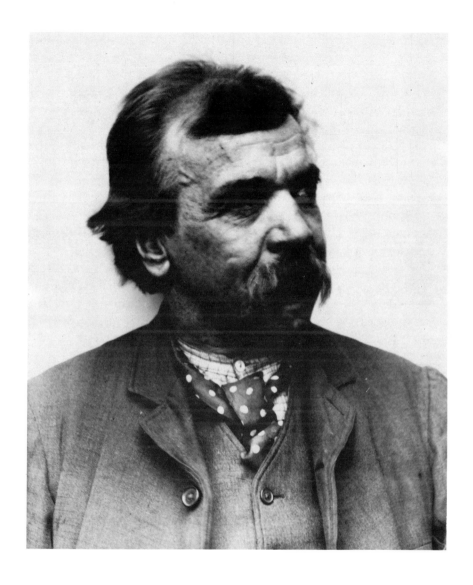

(6)   Bill o' th'Hoylus End photographed in later years.

'Mute are those lips, whose mildest accents spoke
Their sterling worth, down to the harmless joke . . .' etc., etc.

Bill o' th'Hoylus End is seen at his best in his *History o' Haworth Railway*, a humorous embellishment of the assorted rumour, legend and local rivalry attending the building of the Keighley and Worth Valley Railway between 1864 and 1867. In truth, the reality had its ludicrous moments – 'Where be your gibes now, ye wags of Bingley and Cullingworth, your songs, your flashes of merriment, that were wont to set the table on a roar?' A *Keighley News* editorial greeted the completion of the line. 'That decapitated cat, whose martyr end was brought under our editorial notice every other week, is doomed to forgetfulness; Keighley wits will no longer fling her to and fro by the tail . . . The burning and shining lights of Oakworth and Oxenhope, of Flappit, Wilsden, and Harden, will listen in vain for the concussions of oven doors to echo down the steep street and vibrate over the contiguous moors.'

Bill o' th'Hoylus's version abounds with telling sketches of people and events: the Flappeters, 'and strappin folk they are yo mind, sum as fat as pigs, wi heads as red as carrots, and nimble as a India-rubber bouncer taw' . . . the bellman crying a public notice, 'which he did to such a pitch, wal he'd summat to do to keep his hat fra flyin off, but he manijed to do it at last to a nicety, for the news spread like sparks aht of a bakehus chimla' . . . the women who 'held their tungs to that pain and misery wal their stockings fell dahn ower their clog tops'.

The same vigour, and the same appreciation of hearty people, animates the better verses of Bill o' th'Hoylus End:

'I've been i' lots o' feeds, mi lads,
An' hed some rare tucks-aght;
Blood-puddin days with killin' pigs,
Minch pies an' thumpin' tarts;
But I wired in, an' reight an' all,
An' supp'd when I wor dry,
Fer I wor dinin' wi' a gentleman
O' gooise an' giblet pie . . .'

The Politician:

'PIE' LEACH

In the New Year of 1882, in the boardroom at the Keighley workhouse, the Board of Guardians were discussing the treatment of vagrants. Repeatedly one of their members, a man in his later sixties, interrupted his colleagues with 'What a piece of bosh!' and similar expressions, till the meeting became 'very turbulent'.

'Mr Middlebrook said that if Mr Leach did not hold his tongue he would, by the sanction of the Board, put him out of the room.

Mr Leach: "You will not; you cannot."

Mr Middlebrook: "I will try."

Mr Leach: "You will have to get assistance."

Mr Middlebrook: "You are a shame and disgrace to the town and to the Board." '

But what the local press called an 'Extraordinary Scene' came towards the close of the proceedings, when Mr Leach stood in the doorway shouting and gesticulating: 'He was approached by Mr Snowden, the chairman, who asked him to either go in or out of the room. Mr Leach refused and took hold of Mr Snowden by the coat collar, whereupon the two closed together, and in the course of a short scuffle Mr Leach was thrown on his back on the floor by the chairman, much to the amusement of the other members . . .'

In essence, James Leach was a rough-and-ready early Victorian whose forthright personality ill-fitted the more staid circumstances of the later Victorians. He had been born in 1815 at Harewood Hill, near Oakworth, the oldest of five children to 'humble but respectable parents'. His earlier years suggest an entrepreneurial nature seeking a livelihood by whatever means. He worked as handloom-weaver and woolcomber. He helped sink an unsuccessful coal pit near Bogthorn, kept a beerhouse, made leaden spoons, carried by horse and cart to Bradford. He tried gambling and hawking ('he would buy or swop anything,' said his obituary, 'from an oven tin to a steam boiler or from a hedgehog to an elephant'). Briefly he was a travelling showman with a box organ and a shark which had been stranded in the Humber, he had bought it in Hull and had it cured. He served five years as a constable, had a job for a time on Liverpool docks, and with his wife made and sold pies. Keighley would remember him as 'Pie' Leach.

(7)   James 'Pie' Leach in old age.

'Foak called me a' idle un,' he was wont to remark, 'but idle uns oft mak' t'best aat i' money matters.'

This was the man who in middle life, having married a second wife with her own greengrocery shop, burst enthusiastically into local politics. His activities are listed on the elaborate tombstone he had prepared before his death: 'He was elected a member of the Keighley Local Board, and served about 12 years; he was elected a member of the Keighley Board of Guardians, and served 7 years; he was elected a member of the Keighley School Board, and served 2 years; he was elected a member of the Keighley Burial Board, and served 3 years; he was a Commissioner of the Baths and Washhouses for 7 years; and moved the resolution for the incorporation of the town officially in the Finance and General Purposes Committee of the old Local Board of Health.'

His tombstone dutifully records, too, his service from 1848 to 1853 as a Keighley policeman, including his glowing testimonial for 'sober and steady habits'; although, to be precise, he was technically a watchman employed by the Keighley Improvement Commissioners, whose minutes reveal that he was brusquely given a fortnight's notice and discharged! Yet he must have grown widely experienced in the seamier side of town life, watching the late-night taverns, controlling drunks, prostitutes and vagrants, breaking up free fights and 'Irish rows'.

A diary which Leach kept at this time recalls some forgotten notorieties. There was Paul Lad, and 'a person who is comonley caled Red from Kildwick'; John Hey, 'comonley caled Bony Boy', forever 'kicking up a great disturbance' with his wife in the Pinfold; and Samuel Smith, 'comonley caled Mucky Sam', who 'threw Patrick Waterhouse over the batlment at Damside a depth of 5 yards and cut and wounded im daingerousley'.

This was the colloquial, combative atmosphere which James Leach brought into public affairs. In 1872, for example, he was a member of a deputation from the Keighley Local Board which went to London on business relating to the erection of a railway bridge at the station. When they were ushered into the Law Offices of the Houses of Parliament, Leach delivered the following speech: 'We're bahn ter build a brig ower t'railway, an' we think it's nowt but reight 'at we sud hev it. Ther's lots o' horses been lamed at t'level crossing. Why, I wor varry near being jiggered mysel one neet,' What the London gentlemen thought of this we shall never know, but eventually the bridge was built!

On his return to Keighley, Leach lectured for three nights about his adventures in London. The Temperance Hall was crowded, the local press reporting him verbatim in what amounted to a dialect tour de force. 'Pie' depicted himself as a bewildered provincial in the great city: his hotel was 't'biggest public-hahse 'at iver ah wor in', where 'we hed such things at t'table, too, as ah nivver saw. Thar wor a soart of a white clout twizzled up to a point, an' a bun i' t'middle on it, fur ivery one on us. Ah wor capp'd whativer to du wi' this, but ah watch'd tuthers, an' ah gat into t'way i' time. They said ah mud spread it ower mi knees i' this form, then, if owt tummled off a mi' plaate, this little clout wud catch it. An' soa we fan'd t'road in a bit.'

The future Sir Isaac Holden was chairman that first night. In the words of an eye-witness, he 'looked as if he would have liked to drop through the stage'. He did not act as Leach's chairman thereafter.

Neither was the political opposition impressed. The episode occasioned a hostile broadsheet of verses entitled *Leach in London:*
> 'But this worthy old sinner we must give him credit,
> For what he saw there, in his lectures he said it;
> And which of us know but them that went wi' him,
> Were ten times more foolish could we nobut see 'em.'

Politically 'Pie' Leach courted the epithet 'the people's oracle'. His contemporaries would stress his 'defiance of authority', his 'utter disregard of the conventions of society', and his 'wholesome' approach to the ready-made Aunt Sally of public expenditure. He was not always consistent: he became a Commissioner for the Baths and Washhouses although he had opposed their introduction, and sat on the School Board although realising that 'his defective education unfitted him' for the position. Despite having 'moved the resolution for the incorporation of the town', and getting himself nominated as a candidate in five different wards at Keighley's first Municipal Elections in 1882, he was defeated in them all. The town was growing too sophisticated for the likes of 'Pie' Leach.

His personal life too had its droll side. When he grew more prosperous as a greengrocer, he built Balmoral House in Skipton Road, whereon to this day a stone inscription high on the wall pays characteristic tribute to his matrimonial and business dealings: 'These buildings were erected by James Leach, Esq., greengrocer, and Sarah, his wife, of 31, Low Street, Keighley, 1869. Also our Sarah told me, James Leach, that she paid 480 pounds, for house and shop, 31, Low Street, Keighley, in 1840. She died August 19th, 1889. The premises were sold in October, 1889, for 1950 pounds, and was very cheap I think indeed.'

The death of Sarah, Leach's second wife, was followed by an

(8) 'Pie' Leach, the figure on the right, in front of the Keighley Mechanics' Institute. A clock would be added to its tower in 1892.

exhibition even droller than his London lectures. 'Two Funeral Sermons will be preached by James Leach, Esq., of Sandywood Villas, 86, North Street, in the Temperance Hall, Keighley, on Wednesday, February 19th, 1890,' he advertised. 'Between the First and Second Sermon a short Interval will take place, in order to allow those who may feel disposed, to leave the room quietly.'

Again his 'sermons' were reported verbatim. A sample about his second wife illustrates his style of oratory: 'Ah've heeard her say monny a time, in a bit o' nonsense, she nivver missed her way but once, and that wor when she took me (laughter). They called her stepfather John Phillips. He wor a Shropshire man, but they nivver knew where he came fra (loud laughter). You hev t'wrong idea. Ah mean to say what part of Shropshire. Ye laugh before ther's owt to laugh at, but I'd rather ye laughed nor cried . . .'

Leach had been purchasing his own grave space, and planning his own distinctive tombstone, as early as 1889, but he was far from dispirited. In 1892, approaching his seventy-eighth year, he married a third wife. This time she was his new housekeeper, aged thirty-five. The wedding wrote another flamboyant page in the history of his period. A crowd estimated in hundreds filled the road before the Registry Office, sightseers climbing on to window-sills and the roof of a stationary tram. A cheering mob surged round the bridegroom, and his cab-door got torn off. When the noise could be quietened, Bill o' th'Hoylus End recited one of his poems, 'Come, nivver dee i' thi shell, owd lad.'

James 'Pie' Leach died at last on 13th October, 1893.

The Entrepreneur:

ABRAHAM KERSHAW

In September, 1898, Riviere's Grand Orchestra gave some concerts at the Morecambe Winter Gardens. Amongst classics and popular music of the day, Chopin and Auber and Cellier, appeared several valses, *Les Promenades,* by Wahsreka. You may search any number of musical biographies yet find no trace of Wahsreka. This is his story . . .

About 1870, Keighley, not necessarily worse than many a raw West Riding town, 'stood very low in the estimation of the theatrical profession.' Such travelling companies as 'had the hardihood' to appear performed to mostly empty benches in the Drill Hall. In Market Street, one Joseph Bainton was running the Britannia Music Hall on a basic fare of comic songs and boxing matches. Custom was drummed up by such expedients as giving free cigars to the first fifty patrons, awarding a mock-silver watch to the drawer of a lucky number out of a bag, and the wholesale throwing of mousetraps and tin-whistles amongst the audience.

To Keighley at this time came a young pianoforte tuner from Milnsbridge, near Huddersfield. His name was Abraham Kershaw and he nourished an intense interest in the stage. This found an initial outlet in playing the piano in the evenings at the Britannia Music Hall. Indeed, 'Mr Kershaw was the whole band at that time,' a contemporary would recall, 'for he played the piano with his hands and the cymbal, drum, and triangle with his feet.'

Demonstrably, fortunes were not made in this way. Eventually Abraham Kershaw had to sue Joseph Bainton for £10.11s.3d. arrears of wages. He won his case, but 'Mr Bainton said he was out of everything just then.'

The energies of Abraham Kershaw broke out, however, in various directions. He supplemented his piano-tuning with selling music and giving piano lessons, perfectly dove-tailed occupations. A notebook survives: a Miss Butterfield, for example, paid 15s. for twelve lessons, with music 3s. extra, whilst Miss Lucy Greenwood had four lessons for 6s.9d., music 2s.9d.

In 1873, half a dozen citizens formed a Keighley Concert Hall Company Limited, an impressive name with little behind it except the indefatigable Abraham Kershaw. He became secretary, then manager, on the Company's account, of the Britannia Hall; and quite soon, when the rest backed out, proprietor. He operated under the soubriquet Kershaw's Varieties.

'The entertainments at this place will be pleasantly remembered by many,' it would be later stated, 'not perhaps so much on account of their excellence as their delightfully free and easy character.' Be that as it may, one of the turns was a youthful Dan Leno, as a clog dancer.

Another aspect of Abraham Kershaw now became apparent. 'A few Reasons why the Entertainment-going Public of Keighley should Patronise and Support the Varieties Music Hall,' he proclaimed in ringing tones. They were significant reasons: 'Because the Entertainments are arranged to be both classical, comical, moral and instructive, to suit all tastes . . . Because they are provided at a cheap rate, to allow the people who require amusement (the Working classes) the advantage of attending . . . Because the Entertainments are well conducted, with a special regard to the cultivation of good morals . . . Because you get home sober, and to bed at a reasonable hour, and rise in the morning with a clear head, light heart, and pleasant food for reflection, which will cheer you on through your days work, thereby lightening the burden of the same, and saving you an amount of exhaustion.'

It was a far cry from the rough-and-tumble of Joseph Bainton's day. Anybody creating a disturbance could expect to be 'expelled from the Hall, or given into the hands of the Police'.

The eccentric world of mid-Victorian varieties peers out from the advertisements which the likes of Abraham Kershaw inserted in the stage press – advertisements which compensated for the smallness of their print by the burdens they placed upon a groaning English language: 'Artists of Ability are requested to write, stating lowest business terms, which to facilitate, it is requested to be known that Keighley is only Nine Miles from Bradford, Twelve from Halifax, Fifteen from Leeds, Eighteen from Huddersfield, being an easy break for parties passing to and from these towns . . .'

Abraham Kershaw issued announcements couched in period patois ('No use making such big strokes when writing screw; the present state of trade won't allow of it'), and others trying to settle scores ('Would be glad to receive a trifle towards the amount owing to me from J.B. or present address' – this was Joseph Bainton who still hadn't paid up), and some requesting what in any other field would have seemed highly unlikely ('Wanted for Twelve Nights, a good

Sentimental Lady, a good Highland Dancer, Lady or Gentleman, Comic Man (to play Old Woman), and a good Scotch Comic, to assist in the production of *'The Gathering of the Clans'*).

What Kershaw's Varieties actually got was Miss Marian Constance's Great Transformation Skipping Rope Dances, and Alexander Day, the only One-armed Solo Cornet Player in the Profession; Miss Lizzie Dora, the Little Gem, and Rivalli, the Fire Prince; Danvers and Clarence with their clever Dog King Crystal, and Blitz, the Wondrous Plate Expert and Manipulator and Spiral Plate and Pyramid Ascensionist.

In 1877, although still running a music shop, to which he had added a shipping agency, Abraham Kershaw transferred his entrepreneurial talents to the Bradford Star Music Hall, which he managed for several years. Again prospective artists were enjoined to 'remember the depressed trade of the country, and name lowest actual terms'; and again he scooped a young Vesta Tilley.

Meanwhile, Abraham Kershaw had been building a theatre in Keighley. Decidedly this was neither an easy undertaking – it took him four years – nor a safe one. A Mr and Mrs John Billington (artistes of calibre) opined that 'anyone who contemplated building a theatre in Keighley had better give their money away and enter the Workhouse', but Abraham Kershaw persevered. The authorities meddled with his plans. He had to turn a deaf ear to religious bigotry. Some opposed his theatre as 'a great nuisance in the neighbourhood'. Yet at Easter in 1880 his Queen's Theatre and Opera House opened. It was built 'on the American principle', of wood, five storeys high, to seat a couple of thousand.

But it seemed, after all, that the Billingtons might have been right, the opening performance took only £8.3s.6d. towards expenses of £15, and a second season lost £30 in its first week. By 1881, Abraham Kershaw was asking for a reduction in his rates. When this was refused, he rented his theatre for a while to the Salvation Army whereby, as a place of worship, it was exempt from rates and taxes!

After a few years, however, the Queen's Theatre and Opera House settled into a steady if unspectacular routine. Its standard of dramatic fare can be gleaned by the titles: *A Woman's Wrongs, False Lights, Passion's Slave, The Black Flag,* (the latter 'as indicated by its title, deals with life at Portland convict establishment, and includes an escape from that penal settlement, with the hoisting of a black flag'). Occasionally there were cultural treats like *Richard III* and *School for Scandal* and *She Stoops to Conquer,* and the Tichborne Claimant gave an 'interesting Discourse upon his late Trial'. A notebook of gross takings reveals that *Mad Passion* attracted only £30 in a week, *Exiled* £32, *Bells of Fate* £52. The popular *Grip of Iron,* which ran in three successive years, took £120, £112 and £110 respectively; whilst the biggest money-spinner was *Dick Whittington* at £171.

Pantomimes were always favourites. Abraham Kershaw, who amongst everything else had got himself elected to the Keighley Board of Guardians, habitually treated Workhouse children to his Christmas pantomimes, and in 1885 eighty adult inmates, accompanied by the Master and Matron, were thrilled by *Cinderella.*

And all the while, Abraham Kershaw had yet another string to his bow: he composed under the pseudonym Wahsreka, which was A. Kershaw spelt backwards! *The Borough Valse* for piano and cornet, which he dedicated to Keighley's first Mayoress in 1882, was described at the time as 'rather quaint'. Its introduction showed 'a touch of the sacred about it, leading on to one or two pleasing melodies'. The opening lines of his *Pet of St. James's Park* will suffice to illustrate his lyrical style:

> 'I've just arrived from the Strand,
> That's the place for fashions grand;
> Us girls we drive our four-in-hand,
> And lead a jolly life . . .'

In 1887 Abraham Kershaw sold up his Keighley interests. He implied that his music shop was a declining business, but the buyer, William Henry Burns, would develop it successfully, and moved to Morecambe. Within a short time he had become that not uncommon specimen, 'a Morecambised Yorkshireman'. He speculated in property, shops and an arcade, and built Assembly Rooms which he ran as an 'entertaining hall'. During a coal strike in 1893, he lent his Assembly Rooms free of charge for a Grand Concert in aid of deprived children. 'This Appeal is apart from all questions as to the rights or wrongs of the Strike,' he forthrightly emphasised. 'Children are crying for Bread!'

In politics a Liberal, by 1890 and again the following year he stood at the Local Board elections. As enthusiastic as ever, Abraham Kershaw was a committed exponent of Morecambe's holiday potential. He favoured extending the promenade to Bare, with a good road onward to Hest Bank. 'We should then have one of the finest marine drives in the kingdom, and it would give greater facilities for parties driving round the bay,' he told voters, 'thereby inducing more tourists to make Morecambe their centre.' Morecambe, he felt, should 'draw the attention of holiday-seekers and invalids to its superior physical attractions and many advantages over other seaside places as a

(9)   Keighley's New Queen's Theatre between the wars.

(10   One of the travelling variety turns of the 1870s, from a scrapbook of advertisements and letterheads compiled by Abraham Kershaw, Professor Hiodini.

PROFESSOR HIODINI.

THE WIZARD OF THE AGE. [REGISTERED

summer and winter health and pleasure resort.'

His wife too, Louisa Kershaw from Brighouse, became active in Morecambe. In 1898 she was nominated for the Lancaster Board of Guardians, being deeply conscious that out of more than forty members only three were women. Subsequently she became President of the Morecambe Women's Liberal Association, dedicated to 'the requirements of women, socially and politically'.

But Keighley had not forgotten Abraham Kershaw, for he was invited to be a partner in the building of a New Queen's Theatre and Opera House on the site of his old one. This 'exceedingly handsome play-house' by Frank Matcham, the great theatre architect, opened in 1900 before an audience that included 'many of the gentry of the district'.

The Boer War was then waging, and typically Abraham Kershaw donated his first-night takings to the Keighley and District Patriotic and Hospital Funds. There were several topical additions to the concert by some Kentucky Amateur Minstrels and a Mandoline, Banjo and Guitar Band: a Surgeon-Captain Gabriel recited Kipling's *The Absent-Minded Beggar,* the band played *Soldiers of the Queen,* and Church Brigade lads passed round tambourines to collect an extra £36.4s.

Interviewed about this period, some words of Abraham Kershaw are worth remembering: 'In his opinion, healthy recreations and amusements for the people were just as essential as light and air, and his idea was that a well-conducted theatre provided one of the most rational amusements we possessed.'

He was suffering from heart trouble now, but still game to stand on behalf of a Ratepayers' Committee at the Morecambe Borough Bye-Election of 1902. He was still pressing Morecambe's tourist advantages, this time a Poulton Bridge Improvement Scheme provided his special concern, though he did not win. His election address still had an old theatrical ring to it: 'Fewer Promises and Better Performances . . . Less Nonsense and More Serious Business.'

Abraham Kershaw died in 1906, aged sixty-three. He had not had a particularly long life, but it had certainly been a busy one.

The Prima Donna:

MATILDA FLORELLA ILLINGWORTH

'Gia abbiamo nel nostro giornale ripetutamente tenuto parola della giovine prima donna Matilda Florella – We have repeatedly referred to the young prima donna Matilda Florella who, in the past season at Novara, has aroused enthusiasm in that theatre,' the Italian newspaper flowed mellifluously along, that August of 1867. 'Everyone will admire the strength of range, the perfect quality of tone, the feeling with which she interprets music and drama . . .'

It was all a very far cry indeed from Cabbage Fold, Keighley, where she had been born plain Matilda Illingworth in 1843, her father a mill bookkeeper, her mother a dressmaker, and her older sisters power-loom weavers in worsted factories. Her quick metamorphosis to Madame Matilda Florella Illingworth, darling of European opera-houses, and her equally sudden relapse into obscurity, recall some Victorian homily on the fickleness of fortune.

Matilda Illingworth's girlhood remains scantily documented. We know that she 'at an early age gave evidence of a musical talent'; that she joined the Keighley branch of the Bradford Festival Choral Society where her soprano voice became 'more than ordinarily noticeable'; that she shone in such provincial occasions as concerts in aid of the Turkish Bath Company; that a number of local gentlemen 'interested themselves' on her behalf and sent her to the Royal Conservatoire at Brussels. Indeed, a letter survives from one of them, manufacturer John Greenwood of Swarcliffe Hall, near Ripon: he was lending her £10 'to start with' in 1864, and opined that it was 'always well to hope for the brightest things, and altho' I fear only a few out of the many really succeed, you will I hope be of the lucky few'.

More to the purpose, perhaps, is a testimonial written by her professor of Singing at Brussels to 'the parties interested in Miss Illingworth'. She was, he said, an 'excellent' pupil, 'one of the most intelligent' of those he taught, working with 'extreme zeal'. The professor felt personally interested in her, and was giving her all the private lessons she wanted, 'for these she can pay me when she has made some money'. At the Conservatoire pupils' annual competition of 1862, she won first prize.

By the time she returned to a benefit concert in her home town,

(11) Matilda Florella Illingworth as Amina in 'La Sonnambula', a photograph taken during her heyday in Novara, Italy.

early in 1865, she was being triumphantly billed as 'prima donna from the Royal English Opera, Covent Garden'; she had also acquired the name Florella. 'Hundreds of fashionable people' flocked to the Mechanics' Institute to applaud her selections from Auber's *Masaniello* and *Les Diamants de la Couronne* and Donizetti's *Linda di Chamounix*. A duly impressed Keighley branch of the Bradford Festival Choral Society was at least able to accompany her in 'Home, Sweet Home'.

There followed six scintillating years, of advanced study at Milan and of success in Germany and Italy. An older sister, Hannah Maria, left her worsted weaving to accompany the prima donna around the continent. One of Florella's letters to her mother, written from Palermo in December, 1867, reveals their pluck and determination, together with the courtesies and the dangers surrounding young Englishwomen travelling unattended in the troubled era of Italy's Risorgimento:

'We have at last arrived quite safe at Palermo after a voyage of nearly six days. We had to stay nearly two days at Naples on our way to wait for the vessel. I assure you we have been tossed about rarely since last Saturday that we started.

'On board there was an English gentleman who lives at Palermo, he was exceedingly kind to us. On our arrival his gig was awaiting him and he kindly offered it for our use for the purpose of transporting our luggage to the hotel so that we had nothing to pay for that. He also spoke a word to the superior official of the Custom house so that our boxes were not inspected. We came across in a little boat with him to land, and he paid all.

'Travelling from Milan to Genoa by rail, we had very good and most respectable company in our Carriage, one was a Titled gentleman an Italian, the other a Colonel in the Army a Spaniard both of which were most kind. On our arrival at Genoa a sea port town from whence we had to embark, the baron recommended us to the care of the Colonel, & he saw us safe on board . . . You have no idea how difficult it is arriving in a sea port town two girls alone, without a protector, they impose upon us so much, you would scarcely have known me could you have seen me as cross as a wasp chattering Italian with a boat man who had to take us across to the great vessel, he wanted double I would not give it to him . . .'

By 1867, Italian newspapers *La Fama, La Verita, Giornale di Novara* were chorusing her praises, especially in her role as Amina in Vincenzo Bellini's 'La Sonnambula'. This was a favourite part with promising operatic sopranos (Adelina Patti had made it her English debut in 1861), yet in Matilda Florrella, the critics enthused, Bellini's 'sublime and passionate music' had found 'a rare interpreter'.

The next time she revisited Keighley, in 1871, public admiration knew no bounds. Lister Marriner's Brass Band, marching past her house on its way to an engagement at the Mechanics' Institute, stopped in the street to serenade her with 'Home, Sweet Home', and another complimentary concert counted the Duke of Devonshire among its patrons. Once more, a 'fashionable and enthusiastic' audience greeted her operatic repertoire with 'rapturous, loud, and long-continued' applause, and the local press waxed eloquent in her adulation: 'Her voice is unquestionably great in compass, and clear and strong in the top notes – their ring being rich and dulcet, and as definite in their outlines as the notes of a silver bell; while her lower range is surprisingly broad and deep in tone, yet perfectly soft and mellow.'

Describing an extract from *La Sonnambula,* a *Keighley News'* reporter included a glowing physical sketch: 'Her face and eyes are essentially of a dramatic type, especially adapted to illustrate the tragic muse. Her dark eyes in the more impassioned passages, overhung by her expressive, lowering brow, strike and grip the spectator with their intense power.' Her concert raised £100.

Next she entered the busy cosmopolitan life of London, still accompanied by sister Hannah Maria. Her old Aunt Robinson, visiting them in 1873 and keeping a chatty diary of her stay, scarcely mentioned Hannah Maria but penned a daily commentary on 'dear Florella' . . . Dear Florella, it seems, had befriended a French Count, a refugee from the aftermath of the Franco-Prussian War and a kind old admirer who had 'done much good in introducing my niece to influential gentlemen . . .' Dear Florella played the piano 'most exquisitely, for a young lady her extempore is indeed touching'; her friends called her 'a brilliant player' and one gentleman had told her she had 'soul at her finger ends . . .' And inevitably, after sundry walking in Regent's Park and shopping along Hampstead Road, it was dear Florella who saw an excited Aunt Robinson off on her train north.

Of gentlemen friends, indeed, Florella had her share, her genteel affairs or flirtations carried on to an elaborate Victorian accompaniment of carte-de-visite portraits, delicate letters, and verses:

'And search the World, I ne'er can find
A Lady who would be more kind
Than you to whom these thanks I send,
With constant hopes to be your friend.'

One devotee rhapsodised; whilst another (with a Welsh name) felt obliged to propose an assignation in French, instructing, 'Répondez en francais, s'il vous plaît' – their rendezvous was to be 'au côté plus près de Regent's Park de l'église située proche de Portland Road Station'. Inescapably one senses, more than a century later, that Matilda Illingworth's youthful brilliance was losing its lustre.

And quite suddenly, in 1881, it snuffed out altogether. That summer her sister died, of smallpox. 'Sacred to the Memory of Hannah Maria Illingworth,' her funeral-card intoned, 'who Departed this Life 27th August, 1881, Aged Forty-Eight Years. Her sorrows are ended, she is now at Rest'; before switching to the brutally graphic: 'Interred in St. Pancras Cemetery at Finchley, in Grave Marked 1 13 E.'

Alone, Madame Matilda Florella Illingworth returned to Keighley to live with her faithful old Aunt Robinson. This time there was no grand benefit concert, though for a while, a short while, there were musical invitations: 'Mr Butterfield's compliments to Miss Mat. Flor. Illingworth and Mrs Robinson, her aunt, and requests the pleasure of their company on Wednesday Evening, the 21st Dec. at 7 o'clock and hopes Miss Illingworth will bring some music with her.' Then presently there was nothing at all: Matilda Florella, it was rumoured, had taken to drink.

When she died at the age of fifty in 1893, the *Keighley News*, which had so ecstatically praised her two decades before, stated baldly that 'at one period of her life she obtained considerable eminence as a soprano vocalist'. The rival '*Keighley Herald*' concluded a brief garbled obituary with a guarded 'from some cause or other her musical career was not a complete success'. The *West Yorkshire Pioneer* noted that for some years she had lived 'a retired life'; and said, alas, that she had been only 'a popular vocalist'.

About the author . . .

Ian Dewhirst was born at Keighley in 1936 and was educated at Keighley Boys' Grammar School and the University of Manchester. After National Service as a Sergeant-Instructor in the Royal Army Educational Corps, he started work in 1960 at Keighley Public Library, where he has been Reference Librarian since 1967. He writes and lectures extensively on local history, and is the compiler of three collections by Hendon Publishing Company, *Old Keighley in Photographs, More Old Keighley in Photographs* and *Keighley in the 1930s and '40s.* His other books include *Gleanings from Victorian Yorkshire* (Ridings Publishing Company, 1972), *Gleanings from Edwardian Yorkshire* (Ridings Publishing Company, 1975) *A History of Keighley* (Keighley Corporation, 1974), *Yorkshire Through the Years* (Batsford, 1975), *The Story of a Nobody* (Mills and Boon, 1980), *You Don't Remember Bananas* (Ridings Publishing Company, 1985), and *Keighley in Old Picture Postcards* (European Library, 1987).